Nominee TVO tribe poet laureate, 2020,

Pidgin and English Presenter.

Memoirs are a genre of books I ha.. ...,
reading. This book is my first official memoir and I'm glad it was my first. As a seasoned writer, Chinedum has written in a manner that made me finish the piece in one sitting. Reading through felt like driving around Badagry and visiting the highlighted places. I basically felt like I was having the experience with him. The stories were delectably painted to give a virtual experience on the end of the reader. I totally relate to some stories. Every Lagos dweller can attest to the escapades we face on Lagos road. Also, we all have had our days of infatuation. I believe readers will reflect on themselves, too, when they go through this piece. This is me writing this review 2 weeks after reading the book. I still remember the tales and it shows the level of impact it had.

As a writer, I enjoy books that remind me of values. Chinedum took us through different shades of himself- innocence, passion, and adventures. I smiled, laughed, grimaced, and had other emotions while I relished the piece. Indeed, home is the best kind of memories one can have. For someone who also lived around Badagry, viewing the pictures inserted in strategic places gave me nostalgia. I have come to appreciate memoirs more and this book has certainly opened the door to my exploration.

Nkem Obiakor

Winner of Miral National Essay Competition, 2018,

Owner of registered literary arts online brand, *Inkem*.

Everyone has a story to tell. However, not everyone is brave enough to tell that story. In Introversions of The Past, Chinedum tells his story without hesitation, presenting seemingly simple life

INTROVERSIONS OF THE PAST: BADAGRY MEMOIRS

EBISIKE CHINEDUM

Contents

Blurbs

Introversions of the past: Badagry Memoirs is a drive towards profound writing. It's been a while I came across such anecdotal mix of short stories and poetry in a brilliant creative intersection!

Soji Cole

Winner of the ANA Prize for Playwriting, 2014,

Winner of the NLNG Nigeria Prize for Literature, 2018.

I tried to pick a favourite part but I could not. What Chinedum has done is to take us along with him on an interesting tour of different parts of his life; history included and I had a pleasant ride. Safe to say I will recommend this book to anyone looking to be entertained and educated.

Esther Chineye Mbabie

Content and Creative writer,

events in a way as to first excite and entertain, and then encourage introspection. With his tales from his athletic efforts to the pursuits of love, all the while painting a vivid picture of what it's like growing up in Badagry, this author uses his skill to highlight just how fascinating our lives can be, if we look past any looming drudgery. Add in the punctuations with his acclaimed poetry and it is easy to conclude that this book is quite the bit of fantastic writing.

Kazeem AbdulWarith Folarin,

Editor-in-Chief, Ultes Write, Volume 4.

Author's Statement

Episodic and autobiographical memories are said to be crucial in recollecting personal experiences and providing a sense of personal history, including shared history with other people. The term "Episodic memory" was first mentioned by an Estonian-Canadian Psychologist and Cognitive Neuroscientist- Endel Tulving in 1972, when he was distinguishing between knowing and remembering. He further went on to define "Knowing" as factual recollection, while "Remembering" as a feeling that is located in the past (episodic). This serves as the primary premise on which this short creative autobiographical compilation is built. It is an overflow of the events etched on my temporal lobes through my early years. It is also factual, with due elements of creativity. All the pieces (except Pizza's Dilemma) have a common location-Badagry; a unique coastal town located between Lagos and the border of Benin Republic. It is an important place in the history of Nigeria, especially with regards to the Trans-Atlantic slave trade of the 19th century and the prominent missionary activities that followed. To many, Badagry is a point of reference when discussing about the first storey building in

Nigeria, the slave trade museum, the first primary school in Nigeria, and a certain Suntan beach, which seems to thrive more during festive periods. It has also been seen as a place where men and women travel through when smuggling vehicles and contrabands, either to Benin Republic or Nigeria. It is a locale where life is lived from a standpoint of history, serving as a potential tourist destination for all. To me, Badagry is my birthplace, and where I saw the rising and setting of the sun for several years. It is truly legendary.

Introversions of the Past: Badagry Memoirs, starts with a journey from Badagry to a place in Lagos known as *Ojuelegba,* describing the events along the way. It continues with other memoirs, making reference to athletics, friendships, Badagry market, love, school shenanigans, radio tales, experiences at the family shop, and a certain memoir with the title "Badagry Memoirs". It comes to a close with an appendage; an interesting experience I had while in the University of Ibadan.

Introversions of the Past: Badagry Memoirs, is for everyone who loves art, history, and creative non-fiction.

To Senu, Sewanu and Sewedo

Sesi, Senami and Sesede.

Badagry Roundabout, Aerial view

Copyright: Shutterstock

Bus Introversion

September 4, 2020.

TWO WEEKS AGO

Journeys from Badagry to other parts of Lagos have always been hectic- from the almost generic bad roads to the ever-present police officers, custom officials, brawny soldiers, and the supposed diligent officers of the Lagos state Traffic Management Authority (just simply say LASTMA). On this dusty Friday morning, I was on my way to Ojuelegba, a well-known area in the city of Lagos. Ojuelegba is a viable link between the Lagos mainland and the island, while connecting surrounding districts of Yaba, Mushin and Surulere. It is a famous place for hustlers, who work from the early hours of the day to the wee hours of the night, making it one of the busiest places in Lagos. The fame of Ojuelegba has also been made widespread by songs like *Ojuelegba* by Wizkid, Oritse Femi's *Double Wahala* and the legendary Fela Anikulapo Kuti's album, titled *Confusion*.

Back to my journey

I first had to get to a place called Mile-2 before going to Oshodi, where I would board a bus going to Ojuelegba (passing through other places like

Anthony, Obanikoro, Onipanu and Fadeyi). The numerous checkpoints by men of the armed forces are quite tiring. They are always seen along Badagry road, as Badagry is a border town between Nigeria and Benin Republic. Using frowning faces and hands on their guns, they stop passenger-buses. They tell the drivers to park well, then they behave like they have spotted contraband goods or illegal immigrants from fellow West African countries.

Oga park well[1], a policeman commands our driver

He say make you park well! [2] Another officer shouts

A brief discussion ensues between four people- the driver, conductor and two policemen

I later saw an exchange of the Nigerian naira, then the officers were appeased.

One of them tells the driver "na you waste your time o, you for don settle us since naw"[3]

They tell the driver that he is *number 17*, this is the number he is going to tell the policemen at the next checkpoint as proof of settlement. The driver and the conductor get into bus, continue the journey, while railing generational curses at the two policemen. For me, I was only wondering how many drivers those officers would extort before midday. I was trying to do the calculation when I remembered how an officer once asked me to get down from a motorcycle because he perceived that I might be an internet fraudster. I had to *shalaye*[4] that I was not into any internet fraud, while praying that I would still sleep on my bed that night. I am still grateful to my Creator that I did not end up behind bars or, worse still, that the policeman was not trigger-happy at that point.

This scenario plays out again with custom officials. The only difference is that the driver did not get to park the bus, as he had told the conductor before time to extend his hand of blessing towards one of the custom officials. I guess the driver did not want to waste time again, knowing that the reason why they are asked to stop at checkpoints is not really because of contraband goods or illegal immigrants, but for actual extortion by men in national security uniforms.

As we left that checkpoint, the elderly woman sitting next to me started talking to the conductor-

These people ehn[5]

Na so so money dem dey look for[6]

God go punish them[7]

Wicked people!

The energetic conductor replied, "Wo, Na so the country be, everybody just dey do their own"[8]

The last line caught my attention, as I recalled how the Nigerian media houses had been buzzing with the happenings in Ondo and Edo states. The time for election had come, and the prominent political parties were making various chess-moves to ensure victory. I remembered how the deputy governor of Ondo state left the current ruling political party of his state for the People's Democratic Party (PDP) because he had a fallout with the governor. It was believed that he wanted to contest in the next governorship election of the state, the same intention of the incumbent governor, who was seeking a second term in office. He went further to contest in the primary election of the PDP in a bid to become their candidate in the upcoming election. He lost that primary election, a situation that made him leave PDP, cross-carpeting to another political party known as Zenith Labour Party (ZLP) in a bid to also be their sole candidate for the election. I do admire his tenacity and passion to serve the great people of Ondo state. The love he has for his people must be truly remarkable. Then, the state of Edo is quite similar, with the incumbent governor moving to the opposition party after a rancour with his supposed godfather. Let me just pause here.

Finally, I get to Mile-2. I get down from the bus, cross over to the other side. The air is literally filled with noise and horns-

Peee peeee!

Oshodi Oshodi!

Mile-12!

Berger!

Ibadan Ibadan Ibadan!

I locate one going to Oshodi. I quickly board it. I sit down at the front together with a fine gentleman who seems to have two filled bags. The bus gradually gets filled up, and my journey from Mile-2 to Oshodi begins. After collection of our transport-fares by the conductor, the fine gentleman next to me gets up, and to my amazement, he starts talking to the passengers about his drug. He calls it the "Number one flusher", saying that it can flush away everything and anything. I was surprised at first, as I thought that he was too well-dressed for this kind of thing, like he should not be selling "Flushers" in a bus. He goes on to sell his drug to interested people, mainly middle-aged men and a few ladies. He captivates the passengers, speaking *Nigerian-Pidgin-English* and Yoruba language with eloquence, while using humorous illustrations to drive home his point. At the end, I did not know whether to be happy or sad at his plight as I still felt that there could be something better for him to do rather than selling drugs in a bus. But what if he had tried the "Something better", and it did not work out for him? It was at this point that the bus got to Oshodi. The bus stops, we all alight, I walk further, and board a bus going to my final destination- Ojuelegba.

The bus taking me to Ojuelegba is the smallest when compared to those I boarded on my way to Mile-2 and Oshodi. The bus moves almost immediately, with Lucky Dube's hit-songs playing in the bus. It gave me an acute nostalgia of how my brother and I used to play *PlayStation 2*, with our sound system blazing collections of songs by- Westlife, Celine Dion, Don Moen, Kenny Rogers, several old school artistes, and of course, Lucky Dube. These songs were morale boosters back then, especially when we played Pro Evolution Soccer (PES) 2010 and PES 2012. To be sincere, I never really understood how I passed the West African Senior School Certificate Examination (WASSCE), even with such a formidable distraction.

We passed through Anthony, Obanikoro, Onipanu and Fadeyi. These places bring back lovely memories, especially a particular place between Onipanu and Fadeyi. Two names – Temiwunmi and Ikechukwu, will always standout whenever I think of that area. They are legends.

Ojuelegba was already at sight, and I could see how busy it was from a distance. Motors moving to

6

and fro, buses all around, people walking, masses talking, the world in swift motion. Everyone gets ready to alight as Lucky Dube's *Back to my root* booms in the bus.

The bus stops. Everyone gets down. I walk further, only to discover a 1000-naira note is missing from my left-sided trouser pocket. It is too late to start looking for the culprit as everyone had dispersed into the crowd. I shake my head, give a deep sigh, and keep walking towards my friend, who has been waving for about a minute.

Ahead, the sun is a fiery mass, the day is at its youth, and life is still good.

---

1 To park the bus in a good position.

2 Insisting that the driver should park the bus.

3 You wasted your time, you should have been out of here earlier if you had given us money.

4 To explain.

5 Emphasizing this particular set of people.

6 They are keen on getting money by extortion.

7 God will punish them.

8 This is how the country is, everyone is involved in dubious acts.

Street Story

After Moyosore Orimoloye's "Social History"

Yesterday,

Under the orange sun

I told Oluwajimi

That the man who sells Painkillers-

In a certain *Mile– 2 to Oshodi bus,*

Is the same man who sells *Okrika* [1]-

On the Streets of Badagry

I told my friend

That we might never see a greater hustler.

---

1 Second-hand clothes.

Topo Roundabout, Badagry

"You are all speedsters in distinct ways, no one is superior or inferior", these were the words of our games master, who was giving us a pep talk before the final training in preparation for an invitational inter-school relay competition at Iworo Ajido Model College, Ebute-Olofin, Badagry. I was an SS2 student then, fast and quite furious. I joined the school relay team in the aftermath of the school inter-house sport which took place when I was in SS1. I always had the inner belief that running was one of the talents that I possessed, and had been seeking for ways to express it as far back as nursery school.

I grew up as a playful child, actively participating in several childhood games. This was my daily passion until the day I fell down while running to see my sister, who at that point, was in primary 6, and also the senior prefect girl of ASCON[1] Staff School, Topo, Badagry. I tried to stand up, but alas! My left hand was broken. I could feel severe pains all over it. Crying was the natural thing a nursery one pupil like me could do at that point. My parents were alerted, while I kept on crying all through. To this day, no one really knows why I was running at that particular moment, as I ended up telling my parents that I was running to get water from the tap, an infant lie I told. This began my formal introduction to the traditional bonesetter, who tried using his expertise to put the bones back in natural positions. Eventually, it turned out to be in futility. The bones seemed to be irreconcilable. I later had to undergo a surgery that year, and carried a Plaster of Paris cast for 3 months for the bones to be united properly. I still recall how happy I was when the doctor removed the cast on that glorious day in Badagry General Hospital. I was overwhelmed with the thought of having to use my left hand once again. I later got to find out from my mum that the incident which led to the bone fracture was actually more spiritual than physical. I was told that my grandmother's death was the real cause of the school accident. She had died days earlier, and my eldest uncle was on his way to tell my father of her demise. I came into my dad's office with my fractured hand just as my uncle came in too. It is widely believed that this phenomenon called *Awuchi* in some parts of Igboland, could be a parting gift from either of the parents or a way of signaling to one of the children, so that the particular child would know and believe the demise of the mother or father. They say that it can either be a good or bad occurrence, and that this *Awuchi* usually happens to the most loved child of the father or mother. What amused me more was that everyone knew what really happened to me except the person that it happened to, just like a dramatic irony in a suspense-filled drama. Mummy also told me that this traditional concept might be one of the reasons why the orthopaedic surgery was successful. She went on to tell me that the bad occurrences usually get better with time, especially if the late father or mother really loved that particular child.

I was still unwavering in my running expeditions. My mother's words "Chinedum, do not play again o, remember what happened to your hand" were regular at dawn and dusk. She went ahead to buy a big water-bottle for me, attempting to find the solution to the lie I told as the reason for running on that fateful day. I continued running, participating in more outdoor activities. I ran my first supervised race in nursery 2, it was in preparation for the biennial inter-house sport competition, my first one on earth. I came first after outrunning 3 other pupils in my sport house, blue house. I remember how Israel Igiebor celebrated with me on my first well known competitive victory. He ran to meet me just as I crossed the finish line. He was in nursey two at that time too, and had just taken first in his own race, just before mine. The teachers were quite happy with me, even though they always asked me if I was still bent on running just before any race began. They were worried that I might fall again, injuring myself in the process. I ended up participating in the relay race of my peers in the inter-house sport competition. My mum came to support me on that day, as I officially began my running exploits. I cannot really recall what position I took on that day, but I am sure that it was not less than third, even though I strongly feel that I came second.

I got older and faster, but I could not break through as one of the fastest students in school. We had faster students who could practically run like horses and cheetahs. I was way off the pecking order, meaning that I had to wait for my time. My time never came again in primary school as I was not fast enough to represent my house in all the remaining inter-house sport competitions. There were the likes of Utom, Emmanuel and a certain student we all knew as Santos. These guys were like gods of speed during my primary school days. They were all my seniors. Utom was considered to be the fastest until the day Emmanuel beat him in a keenly contested race. Santos was in blue house, and was silently watching all that was going on. He had a unique way of running, in the sense that you could always leave him for dead in the early stages of a 100m race, only for him to surprisingly hit you from the 60m mark, as he had a ferocious acceleration to the finish line. Santos outran both

Emmanuel and Utom to finish first in the 100m senior boys' final of my last inter-house sport competition in primary school. He used his usual technique, coming from behind to win the race. Emmanuel came second while Utom came third. I did not get to participate in the next inter-house sport, which was bound to happen when I would be in primary 6, as I had already left for secondary school after primary 5.

I moved on to Badagry Grammar School, or specifically, Badagry Junior Grammar School. I chose to be a day-student rather than stay in the boarding house as home was just close by. I had never imagined that a school could be that big. It was my second stint in a secondary school after briefly going to a school known as Frontline, still in Badagry. I lived most of my days in Frontline with the fear of being flogged, and yes, I was duly beaten, most times for minor collective mistakes, apart from the general noise-making flogging that my classmates and I received daily. There was no real running opportunity in Frontline unlike Badagry Junior Grammar School where I saw students run like international speedsters. The inter-house sport competition of Badagry Junior Grammar School came when I was in JSS1. I was working towards the Junior boys' 100m final. My target was to at least qualify for this race and then hope for the best. I was gradually becoming the person to beat in my house as only two other junior boys gave me tough times during practice. On one of the selection days, I outran every other junior boy that I ran with, prompting the games master of my house to write my name down for the final selection race of the 100m junior boys. That was how I became jittery; I was suddenly scared of what that day could bring. As fast as I was, I was still scared that I would fall short on the last selection day, and that even if I got selected, I might still not be able to compete with the junior boys of other houses. I lacked self-confidence, and this made me to be absent from school on that particular day of the final selection of athletes from different houses. I had no problem convincing my parents that I wanted to stay back at home on that day, as I had earlier told them the truth, that we only play and train on inter-house sport practice days, meaning that no meaningful class would hold. Meanwhile, I had already lost my school shirt, trouser, necktie and my sandals due to careless handling of my school uniform after changing to my sportswear just before a practice session. I came back to school after the final selection day to hear that they had been looking for me throughout the previous day for me to grace the track with my speed. I was further told that they had done the selection and just like I had predicted, Waliu and Chijioke were the two junior students selected to represent red house, my house.

They had both beaten me in a less competitive race, and I already had the feeling that they were actually the two fastest junior boys in my house. This was also one of the reasons why I decided not to come on that selection day. I feared that they might also outrun me again. The finals of the inter-house sport competition was scheduled to hold on the Saturday of that same week.

I attended the finals of the inter-house sport competition with an open mind. I just wanted to see how fast the runners of the Great Badagry Junior Grammar School were. The races were intense, from that of the junior boys and girls to that of our seniors in JSS3. Our house did not do too well in the junior races, Chijioke had an injury that same week and he could not perform up to his best while Waliu seemed to have lost his form. It got worse for us in the senior category as we did not register a single podium finish in all the races. I was quite sad, though I had other moments to savour, like seeing the dreaded games prefect run. He was not the tallest of the senior students, but he had powerful springs of lower limbs. His closest rival was the hostel prefect, who was relatively taller. Unlike a race between Utom, Emmanuel and Santos, in which Utom would be the best starter, while Emmanuel would catch up with him in the middle, leaving Santos to always come from behind to win right at the end of the race, this showdown between the two prefects was however slightly more intense and quite different in style. The games prefect was in green house while the hostel prefect was in yellow house. In the opening stages of the 100m senior boys' final, the two prefects were slightly clear of every other runner. They continued tussling for first position until the games prefect seemed to put in another gear and outran the hostel prefect in a quite majestic manner. The whole school went into a frenzy, especially the junior students who had hardly seen the games prefect run, as they only hear of how fast he could be. The other races and relays were also exciting to watch, though I was not part of it again as I had missed the ultimate selection day, even though I knew that I was fast enough to be part of the junior boys' relay team of my house. The closing highlight for me was the invitational inter-school 4 by 100m relay race. Other schools were called to participate in this relay race, bringing their best runners to the field. It happened that our school also sent runners to participate too. Our relay team for this event consisted of two senior students alongside the hostel and games prefect. That relay race still remains one of the fiercest that I have ever seen. The Senior Secondary School section of Badagry Grammar School was also invited, alongside their own fastest student, popularly called *The beast*. He actually did look like a friendly one, with a hefty upper-body frame and muscular-looking legs. Ajara Grammar School, Ansar-ud-deen Grammar School, Ibereko State High School, Sito Gbethrome Senior Secondary School, and Federal Government College, Ijanikin, were the other schools present. The relay race started with each school having little or no difference at all. Then, at the third leg, it turned out to be between Badagry Junior Grammar School, Badagry Senior Grammar School and Federal Government College, Ijanikin. The race went into the anchor leg, with our games prefect in a close third at this stage, while Badagry Senior Grammar School was leading. Then just as we saw him do it in the 100m final, the games prefect turned the heat on with a moment of sheer brilliance, coming from the rear, and taking first just at the final moment, beating *the beast* of Badagry Senior Grammar School. Everywhere went wild, even our principal could not believe what he saw. He stood up and was shouting at the top of his voice. It was simply out of this world.

I moved on from BJGS to French Village International College, after my parents felt that BJGS was turning me to a very rough and rugged child. I had no option than to obey them. I always missed the friends I made in BJGS, from Abraham who used to tell me of how much he loves Theo Walcott, Arsenal and Dancing Rasta in *Supa Strikas* [2], to Precious who modelled his football style after Cristiano Ronaldo. I still remember the likes of Jimoh, whose funny attributes, football skills and intelligence were remarkable. Onyedikachi was my class captain then, ever reliable in inter-class football matches, the same as Babatunde, Farouk and a certain Chinedu, who was a potent defender. Then, there was Ibrahim, Theophilus and Chukwuma, who later became the senior prefect boy when he got to Badagry Senior Grammar School.

In French Village, I had to study more than I did in BJGS. I tried having good grades while looking for opportunities to play and of course, run. I took my chances as they came, establishing myself as the fastest student in JSS2. I was closely followed by Daniel, who was quite taller. For the JSS3 class, they had Tolu who was also the assistant-senior prefect boy. He was incredibly fast. There was no inter-house sport competition that session, even though I was becoming more confident in my abilities.

I moved on to my final secondary school- Ascension College, Imeke, Badagry. My parents had their undisclosed reason for withdrawing me from French Village international college. I still suspect it was because of the school fees that my siblings complained of. To my siblings, I was paying even more than they were as undergraduates in Nigerian Federal Universities. I passed the written exam and was accepted into Ascension College, with Mr. Adams congratulating me.

Life in Ascension College was quite the same as other schools. I was active in running activities from the very start. I had several rivals at this stage, but I was still able to assert myself as a formidable competitor. After the Junior Secondary School Certificate Examinations, I progressed to SS1. This meant that I had gradually grown into a more athletic student. I was faster than ever at this stage, being among the top three fastest runners in my class, the others being Ayomide and Ahmadu. Ayomide had a very fast start and Ahmadu had longer legs. As at that time, the games prefect was the fastest person in the school, followed by the senior prefect boy. Ayomide's elder brother, Ifedayo, was also among the fastest students in SS3, Bright and Ibrahim were other speedsters of that set. For SS2, Oche, Kenneth, Tunmise and Ajao were too close to really pick the fastest person. Tunmise seemed to get the upper hand the final time that they all ran together in SS2. Oche and Kenneth were more regular in the relay team. They were always on the heels of each other.

The inter-house sport competition that year was filled with the exploits of the senior prefect boy, who practically carried green house all through. He narrowly lost the 100m senior boys' final to the games prefect, who was also in the same house. The nickname of the games prefect of that set was *Okada* [3], signifying the way he runs, springing his short powerful legs in a continuous forward motion. I will never forget seeing the way he outran both Kenneth and Oche in one of the relay races, coming from behind, and making them feel like they were wasting their precious time by trying to beat him. It was another great sight to behold. I took part in the 400m final of that inter-house sport competition, coming last behind the likes of Bright, *Okada*, Kenneth and Ifedayo. Ifedayo won that race.

I became more active in the school relay team by SS2. I started becoming more prominent, flexing my muscles against the likes of Oche, Kenneth and at a point, Tunmise and Ajao, who were all in SS3 at this stage. There were also the likes of Tomiwa and Musa who were in SS1. I was in a way, destined to become the next fastest student by the time I would be in SS3.

On this particular day, we were training for a relay race that was going to be at Iworo Ajido Model College, Badagry. I had been working as hard as I could to get my first shot in an invitational inter-school relay race. I ended up being amongst those who would run. I was happy that my time had finally come. I got prepared and we arrived at the school. There was also another invitational inter-school relay competition that day, meaning that we had to split into two groups, the first group went to Iworo Ajido and the other, to a school known as Supreme Pillars. The likes of Kenneth and Oche went to Supreme Pillars, while Ahmadu, Tomiwa, Adedayo and I went to Iworo-Ajido. I took the third leg of this relay race, beating every other runner that I ran with. I handed the baton over to Tomiwa, who ran alongside the fastest student of Iworo Ajido, it was quite a tough one, with the Iworo Ajido student just edging him out. We finished in second place, signaling the end of my first invitational inter-school relay race. I was quite happy, both personally and collectively. Our female runners also took second place in their own high-octane relay race. I went on to participate in other invitational inter-school relay races, finishing first in all the legs I took, and first collectively too. I was never beaten in a competitive inter-school relay race.

The next year was an inter-house sport year, I had patiently waited for this opportunity. I was already the acclaimed fastest student in the whole school, with very fierce competition from both Ahmadu and Musa, who were also extremely fast. Ayomide had left Ascension College at this point, and I wished that he had stayed to make the competition even fiercer. I was now in SS3, with

Ahmadu, who was in my house, and the labour prefect too. Musa was in SS2, the same as Tomiwa.

The inter-house sport competition came with a blazing start from me, showing everyone that I was unbeatable during all the practice sessions. I was in the form of my life, or so I thought. I ended up making a mistake, one that marred my performance in the later stages. I did not heed to calls that I needed to rest from the numerous races I was running. I eventually began to tire out even before the heats started, a situation that played out well for Musa, who had studied my weakness and used it against me in both the 100m senior boys' heat and final, outrunning me in both races. As for the 200m, I could not even qualify for the final as I came 4th in one of the heats. I even fell during the 4 by 400m relay race, as I kicked the ground while attempting to move into first position during the second leg. This caused my house to come 3rd in that relay race. Things got worse for me in the 100m senior boys' final as I was wrongly given 3rd place, a situation that saw Benjamin, the Physics laboratory prefect take 2nd. I had used "Experience" to run that race, starting as fast as I could in a bid to scare my fellow speedsters. Musa knew me too well though, smelt the blood, and went for the kill. The other runners in the 100m senor boys' finals were- Tomiwa, Enawayon and Sonya. Sonya was the games prefect of my set. He, apart from Mayowa and Kelechi, was very versatile, participating in almost all kinds of games. He had the charisma and razzmatazz of Brazilian samba footballers, with agility, speed and endurance of Kenyan runners. He was a complete athlete and sportsman. On this very day, he did not get to have one of his best races as Musa chased me down to the very end. Other runners had a go too, with Benjamin being the most favoured by God to be given the 2nd place after a mix-up by the official at the line. Benjamin also took first in long jump and had a really good inter-house sport competition. Ahmadu chose to participate in the 200m, I cannot recall the position that he ended up with. For the 4 by 100m relay race, Sonya showed everyone one of the reasons he was the games prefect. He took the anchor leg for his house, and led his team to victory, beating Musa and Ahmadu in the process. I took the third leg for my house, but could not avert the win by Sonya's led yellow house.

My final relay race came in second term of SS3. It was an invitational inter-school relay race. The venue was Supreme Pillars. Our games master chose Tomiwa, Musa, Joshua and I to execute the 4 by 400m relay race. Joshua was a new member of the team who was in SS1 at that point. It was yet another explosive race as we came from behind to have a big win. It is still one of my most memorable moments, as I took the anchor leg and brought home the gold. Tomiwa started the relay race, giving the baton to Joshua, Joshua to Musa, and Musa to me. The distance between us and the other schools was quite large, because the person who should have taken a near second-place fell down during the anchor leg, almost bringing me down with him too.

I went back to Ascension College three years ago to pick up my official West African Senior School Certificate. I went around, looked at the field, walked on it, and then, remembered all those races. I still fight the cruel reality of nature, as it tells me that I will never get to experience the thrills of running in a school race again.

---

1 Administrative Staff College of Nigeria.

2 A popular football-themed comic.

3 A local name for motorcycle.

I.A.A.F.- International Associations of Athletics Federations.

Diamond League- An annual series of elite track and field athletic competitions comprising 15 of the best invitational athletics meetings.

How to win a 100m Race

Start the race like Olusoji Fasuba

Accelerate like Shelly-Ann Fraser-Pryce

Then run like Usain Bolt

From 60m to the finish line.

First Storey Building in Nigeria

Copyright: Premium Times

Shop Cogitations

Last night, I dreamt of the man who comes to buy fifty-naira *garri* [1] and twenty-naira sugar at our shop. He was telling me of how he plans to get married very soon. He even pointed towards a nearby classy event centre, saying that he was going to use that place for his wedding reception. I woke up wondering if he was still dreaming inside my dream. How could he be planning to get married when he barely has enough to feed himself?

Goshen is the name my dad bestowed upon the rented shop. It is located along *Ansar-ud-deen* road, close to Holy Child International School, Badagry. It is part of a sequence of shops on the right side of the road leading to the other part of a place known as *Limca.* My dad named it *Goshen* in relation to the biblical story of the Israelites and Egyptians, where *Goshen* was the place of the Hebrews, and was completely free from the plagues that besieged the other parts of Egypt. In a way, it ultimately proved to be the place of reference for my dad during his contemplations on the names to render to the shop.

Brick-red seems to be the colour of the exterior walls, while the inside of the shop is painted white and green, like the Nigerian flag. The shop is filled with all sorts of food items, ranging from staple foods- rice, beans and *garri,* to items for cooking soup and stew, such as *egusi* [2], *ogbono* [3], crayfish, native salt, ground pepper, palm kernel oil, vegetable oil, ginger, garlic, *maggi* [4], stock fish, onions, tomato pastes, fifty naira eggs, curry, thyme, nutmeg and locust beans. There is also the availability of packs of bottled water and plastic-bottled soft drinks. Other notable items include groundnut, sugar, boxes of matches, packs of toothpicks, and a carton of *indomie* [5] super pack. The design of the shop is such that it allows the use of tables at the front, to allow items such as rice, beans, *garri,* palm kernel oil and vegetable oil to be clearly seen from a distance. There is also a front rope that enables items such as tomato paste, nutmeg, curry, thyme and sachet vegetable oil to be hung.

The left side of *Goshen* is a shop whose owner is a baker. She is a supplier of cakes, puff-puffs, doughnuts, meat pies and sausage rolls to some schools around, as well as baking for several events and ceremonies. She is a hard-working woman whose quality pastries speak volumes of her ability. She is simply known as *Mama Jesuyon.* Towards the right is the shop of a Ghanaian woman who sells alcoholic drinks, dry gins, detergents, sachet milk, sachet water, sweets, and recharge cards. She is popularly known as *Mama Favour,* Favour being the name of her ten-year-old daughter. Her shop is partly a centre for the youths for love the taste of alcohol, and partly for the everyday people who need recharge cards for communication and data purposes.

I come to the shop six days in a week, mainly from twelve P.M. to seven-thirty P.M. I carry my mum's shop bag, inside it are usually two rechargeable lamps and a purse, which contains the key and naira notes. The lamps are for the night, as we made no attempt to connect the shop to any electricity distribution company of the state, Lagos state. I walk about two hundred metres to the shop, this is the distance it is from the house. I usually get to the shop quite fast due to my long strides. At the shop, I start to unlock the padlocks without much stress, paying less attention to the front of the shop, which is a major deviation from the warnings of my parents. My parents always tell me to watch the surroundings of the shop every time I arrive, as it is widely believed that the probability of African black magic in Badagry is the same as the probability of the sun rising and setting within twenty-four hours. The other day, my mum told me of how the woman in one of the adjacent shops appeared to her in her dream, asking about what she was selling, only for my mum to look behind her to find a well packaged red coloured *juju*. My dad also shared his experience, still a dream, of how he saw the same woman coming into *Goshen* through a place that serves as a wall in reality. My dad said that she seemed shocked to find out that she could be seen in that dream, like she never expected to be caught. She is also known by people as someone who engages in fetish things, like coming to buy items from people with tattered money, as a means to spiritually stop other people from coming to buy items from that particular shop. I however, seemed to be undeterred by her presence in this area, always believing that no scheme of man or spirits can shake me, even though I plead the blood of Jesus both day and night on the shop as an insurance.

I completely unlock the shop. I go inside and get the broom to sweep the front of the shop. I do this daily, except on Sundays. I sweep with water on some days to reduce the dust around. Mum always tells me to sweep with water to which native salt has been added. She explains that this helps to cleanse the front of the shop from every evil substance that might have been placed at the front of the shop during the dark hours of the night. I find a way not to do this, or do it rarely, pretending to add the native salt in most cases. After sweeping, I bring out the tables, chairs, and necessary food items to the front of the shop. I then sweep and clean the inside of the shop, arranging the other items. I lay down the mat in the shop on the carpet covered floor. This is where I rest before the customers start coming in their numbers. I finish this routine by washing my hands with *Morning Fresh* liquid soap and well-water that has been brought in a keg from the house. I then lay on the mat, waiting for the customers to start coming.

The customers start coming. A man comes to buy one *pan* of *ajase garri* [7], another buys one-hundred-naira worth of fried groundnut. Ten minutes later, the woman who sells cooked beans in one of the adjacent shops sends her small daughter to buy twenty-naira *maggi* and fifty-naira ground pepper. I sell these items to her. Later, a woman comes to buy three-hundred-naira worth of *ogbono* and two-hundred-naira worth of crayfish. I sell these items too. I come back to lie down on the mat while remembering the day a beautiful lady came to buy *ogbono* from the shop. I was surprised to see her that I ended up giving her seven hundred naira instead of two hundred naira as her change, as I thought that she gave me one thousand naira, whereas she gave me five hundred naira for three-hundred-naira worth of *ogbono.* She is one of the few beautiful ladies to have bought an item from the shop, maybe that is why I still remember her. I still wish to see her again.

Further people come to buy one-hundred-naira palm kernel oil as well as fifty-naira vegetable oil. *Mama Favour* also buys fifty-naira *ajase garri,* and *half-derica*[8] of white beans which is one hundred and twenty-five naira. *Mama Jesuyon* comes to her shop around five P.M. She buys one-thousand-naira vegetable oil for the next day. She does not pay, but tells me to record it for her, that she is going to pay sometime this week. I give her two vegetable oil filled seventy-five centilitre plastic-bottles. I then add the money to her increasing debts. My favourite male customer comes around twenty-seven minutes to six P.M. He buys his usual fifty-naira *garri* and twenty-naira sugar. He then starts to tell me about the goings-on in the nation, about how inflation and corruption is rising, not to forget the instability in the north-east. He goes on to tell me that he is also a graduate of the department of Chemistry from one of the prominent federal universities. He says that he has applied to over ten establishments, each of them saying that they would get back to him. He tells me that he is still waiting for one of them to get back to him. We go on to talk about the latest match of the Super Eagles of Nigeria, talking about the performances of the likes of *Ndidi, Iwobi, Musa, Ola Aina and Victor Osimhen.* He later tells me that he wants to start going home, I tell him "okay naw, we go dey alright"[9]. We shake hands and he goes off.

The time ticks. It gets to three minutes past seven P.M. I put on one of the rechargeable lamps. Neither mum nor dad came to the shop today, as they had both gone to *Oyingbo market* [10] to buy more food items for the shop. They had arrived home around six P.M. The time gets to twenty-four minutes past seven P.M. I start getting ready to go home. I put the mat back together and begin to carry all the displayed food items, tables, and chairs back into the shop. I accomplish this successfully. I then count the money I had gotten for the day. It is one thousand, nine hundred and fifteen-naira. I thank God for it. I put the money back into the purse, and put the purse in my mum's shop bag. Just then, a woman comes to buy one twenty-naira onions, while another buys fifty-naira palm kernel oil and ten-naira native salt. I happily sell these items before locking the shop. I put the key in the purse, and return the purse into the shop bag. I extend my formal night greetings to both *Mama Favour* and *Mama Jesuyon*, who are both around, then, I set home with my mum's shop bag and the rechargeable lamps.

I take a different route back home as the other path would have been occupied by some youths of the town, who usually smoke and drink all sorts of substances. I walk quite briskly to the house while greeting familiar faces on the way. I get to the gate of the house. I knock three times, and await my dad to open the gate. I check the time on my *Nokia torch phone*[11]. It is already four minutes to eight o'clock on this Friday night.

---

1 Dry edible granules made from cassava.

2 Fat-and-protein-rich seeds of cucurbitaceous plants, serving as ingredient in West African meals.

3 Nuts of *Irvingia species*, used as thickening agents for dishes.

4 A food seasoning.

5 A brand of instant noodle.

6 An object that has magical powers.

7 A popular type of *garri*.

8 Half of a *derica,* which is used as a measuring cup for staple foods.

9 We will be just fine.

10 A popular food market in Lagos state, Nigeria.

11 A well-known small phone.

Weekends are glamorous in Yorubaland, from weddings and naming ceremonies, to the sheer frenzy of Lagos markets. Equivocally, it also serves as a rare opportunity for the societal elites and civil servants, to relax and unwind from the busy schedules of the week. Markets are one of those places where *Lagosians* are always seen in great numbers during weekends, from selecting wares to buying several food items for the coming week. In terms of prominence, the likes of *Balogun, Oyingbo, Oshodi, Ladipo, Idumota, Trade fair,* and *Alaba* markets, are more recognized in Lagos state, including a host of others. Far away on the other side of Lagos is the Badagry market, known locally as the *Agbalata* market. It serves as the main market in Badagry, supplying its citizens as well as another region known as *Seme border-* a settlement in Nigeria on the border with Benin Republic. The market is of mixed ethnicity- Yorubas, Igbos, Hausas and the Eguns. It is quite big too, spanning a large land mass. The market comprises several sections for almost everything, including a section for *okrika,* our very affordable second-hand items. There is also an abattoir, which serves as a slaughterhouse for the goats and cattle being sold.

Saturdays are usually very busy for the family. We would wake up to assemble in the parlour as usual, praying to our Father who art in Heaven. Everyone gets to disperse after this, as we would start doing the important house chores and personal hygiene routines. Later, I would be sent to buy the daily bread at *Oropo-* a junction that is roughly around 400m-500m from the house. The breakfast on Saturdays are always eaten quickly. Then, my parents, siblings, and I would get to decide who would "Follow" my parents to the market. The primary purpose for this was to choose the person who would carry all the bags containing all the items bought in the market. It was quite a task, as the person chosen would have to spend close to 3 hours walking with my mum, in and around the market, while carrying the bags. The person would also have to greet my mum's friends in the market, reply some of the market sellers, and sometimes, apologize to some sellers who will feel bad that my mum did not purchase their goods, even after showing keen interest at first. I get picked most times, maybe it is because I am the *baby of the house*[1].

We usually start by buying what we have come to know as "Provisions", the likes of milk, sugar, beverages, *Lipton yellow tea,* tissue paper, toothpaste, and detergent. We would then move to the butchery section, where we would spend time negotiating on the size and cost of a large piece of beef. This is where I always get amazed at my mum's *pricing* skills. She would beat down the price of a sizeable piece of beef from 2,500-naira to 1,000-naira and still get to cajole the butcher to add *jara* [2]. Personally, I would have just bought the piece of meat for the 2,500-naira without even asking if that was the *last price* [3]. Mum loves buying her beef from Hausa butchers, speaking the hausa language to them; I consider this as the major reason why she easily gets large pieces of beef at a reduced price.

We would move further to buy other food items like fresh tomatoes, pepper, onions, plantain, carrots, half crate of egg, *Ijebu garri* [4], palm kernel oil, four tubers of yam and some food spices. We would spend minutes at several spots as we would keep on going around the market, searching for mum's preferred market sellers, or where things could be gotten cheaper. We would then get to my favourite place, the fish seller's place. The fish seller is a woman who captivates me with her cheerful smile. She is light-skinned, and looks to be between 35-40 years of age. There is a calm receptive nature about her that always makes me look forward to going to her place, or at least, seeing her. Mum usually buys 1,000-1,500-naira worth of fish from her. She would then get to say "Mummy

mummy, Thank you o". I always smile whenever she says this, just as mum does too.

Our regular final point before going home is a shop whose owner is known as *Mama Ada*. She is a long-term friend of my mum, selling all sorts of soup ingredients and vegetables, from *okazi* to *egusi, ogbono, ugu, green,* stockfish, crayfish, scent leaf, bitter leaf, and a whole lot more. This is where my mum comes to buy all her soup ingredients, depending on the particular soup to be prepared. *Mama Ada* is an Igbo woman who lives with her family in Badagry. She is known by her first daughter, *Ada,* who is as beautiful as her mother. My mum would get to discuss with her on different topics, ranging from the varying cost of bride prices in Igboland, to how water *use to enter Mama Ada's house* due to the flood from heavy downpours. Their conversations would go on and on until *Mama Ada* would give my mum the ordered soup ingredients and vegetables, usually sliced *ugu*, stockfish, scent leaf and *okazi.* We would also get to grind some items at a nearby distance to her shop. The person who helps us to grind our items is usually my namesake without the letter 'm' at the end of his name, simply put, his name is *Chinedu* not *Chinedum.*

We would start going home at around 2pm, having been in the market for about 2 hours and 45 minutes. All this while, my dad would be waiting for us in the car. My mum and I would find a way to locate and enter the car. I would also get to put all the bags into the boot, and we would eventually start our short trip back home. On arrival, everyone would get to help in bringing out, sorting and arranging the bought items. Then, we would all get to eat either *Indomie noodles* or any food that was available before we left for the market, and later prepare for a proper meal.

---

1 The youngest child of a family.

2 Extra amounts/portions of something bought, usually added by the seller.

3 The final price of an item before purchase.

4 A type of *garri* (gotten from cassava).

There was a time I never missed an episode of *Story, Story: Voices from the market.* The BBC radio drama was first aired on 20 radio stations, expanding to 164 radio stations worldwide as at 2017. I listened to each episode every evening on Wednesdays on *Raypower 100.5 FM Lagos.* I still remember the characters of this drama series, the likes of Mr. Montu, Chief Santos, John Bosco, Ejike, Tami, Chairman Rasheed, Linus Igbokwe, Mama Risi, Madam Fati, Jude, Mallam Bello, Frank, and some other voices from the market. It was the first radio drama I was exposed to, and it was worth every bit of my time. It proved to be extremely entertaining, providing humour mainly from the likes of Linus Igbokwe, Ejike, Mallam Bello and the grandiloquent Jude, who taught me how to use "Affirmative" instead of yes, and *Picanini* instead of saying "Fine girl". This radio soap opera also brought societal issues to the fore, ranging from motor park crises to political hostilities, local government brouhahas, marital struggles, environmental sustainability, HIV/AIDS awareness, and all sorts of problems from the local market. A masterpiece is what I have come to tag this highly interesting and relatable radio drama, which was created by the BBC Media Action in 2003.

I was also intrigued by another radio drama called *Straight from the Heart* on the same radio station, this time, it was aired every Saturday morning. This highly emotional radio drama was usually accompanied by one of Bryan Adam's songs; the title of that song was the same as the title of the radio drama. *Straight from the Heart* mainly focused on relationship issues, the likes of heart breaks, sexual abuse and domestic violence. I tried to always listen to it, either at home or on my way to the market on Saturdays. This radio drama also formed part of my perceptions of love, and issues of inhumanity to humans, particularly to females.

I was always on the search of radio programmes, switching from one radio station to another. Most times, I was hoping to find a random sport programme. I stayed with *Raypower 100.5 FM Lagos* for a while, getting used to the different schedules for the different days of the week. I could tell when *Planete Musicale* was coming up on a Thursday, and when *BBC World Sport* from the BBC World Service Radio would take over on some days of the week, with the voice of Oluwashina Okeleji being my favourite. I also knew the daily morning programmes of this radio station and even the periods when the World News would be disseminated. I cannot forget *Fact File, Frankly Speaking with Muyiwa Afolabi,* and the *Political Platform* crew. There was also a weekly inspirational programme which I hardly missed, and a very exciting sport show every Saturday morning by 9am. I could go on and on to write about how Thursdays were for old school music, how Okechukwu Eze seemed like the most popular radio newscaster together with Abiola Aberuagba, and how DJ Jimmy Jatt and DJ Neptune all worked with *Raypower 100.5 FM Lagos.*

I encountered other radio stations along the way, the likes of *Metro FM, Radio Continental, Brila FM, Cool FM, Classic FM, Wazobia FM* and *Nigeria info FM,* which later turned out to be my favourite radio station. I got to know Metro FM with frequency 97.6MHz FM (now 97.7MHz FM) through a sport programme known as *Sport Summit,* which used to air from 1pm to 2pm every Monday to Friday. It was hosted by Kelechi Bernard, with support from the likes of Godwin Enakhena and Charles Anazodo, who went on to work with the sport crew of the *Multichoice Group*-the owners of *DStv, GOtv* and *Showmax.* I still remember that Kelechi Bernard was, and is still an astute FC Barcelona fan. It was here that I got to get several analyses on football, tennis, basketball, and other sports, including cycling and *Formula One.* I always loved the analyses of Godwin Enakhena, as he seemed to give out his wealth of experience every time he analyzed issues pertaining to the national teams, the Nigerian Professional Football League, and the problems facing sports development in the country. Femi Farawe and Adeniyi Kunu later joined the *Sport Summit* crew. Comfort Agbai usually takes over from here by 2pm. She played lovely songs. It was during one of her shows that I heard *C'est la vie,* a French song by Henri Dikongue, a Cameroonian singer and guitarist. I also followed a particular quiz show for secondary school students every Saturday morning. I could never forget how coordinated the network news on the network service of Radio Nigeria was, as Metro FM joined them for the news on certain hours of the day.

Radio Continental (102.3 MHz FM) provided me with great humour at the later hours of the day with the likes of *Wale Powpowpow, Iya Jogbo, Danbaba* and *Tatafo* (Helen Paul), combining to form a very dramatic and comical show known as *Wetin Dey. Radio Continental* is now known as *Max FM. Brila FM* (88.9 MHz FM) gave me live details of the *Super Eagles* matches on days when there was no electricity supply from the Power Holding Company of Nigeria, with no plans to turn on the *Tiger* generator. Cool FM (96.9 MHz FM) and Classic FM (97.3 MHz FM) provided me with more music. Cool FM was good with different genres of music while Classic FM dealt more with several old school songs. Wazobia FM (95.1 MHz

FM) was always there for the soothing talk shows and of course, the consistent use of *Nigerian-Pidgin-English. Nigeria info* (99.3 MHz FM) proved to be my last stop before I got admission to the university. I discovered it in 2013 though I cannot vividly remember the particular show I first listened to on this radio station. I loved hearing the likes of Adenike, Tolulope Adeleru-Balogun, Zoe Chinaka, Onome, Chuks Ene, and Wemimo Adewuni. There was also the *Alibaba seriously* crew which had the likes of *Olwabibs, The Guvnor,* Ifeanyi, *Lafup, Sir Jeff, MC Prince* (now *Mr. Hyenana*) and *Alibaba.* There was this constant caller known as *Obaro* who used to talk at length during this programme, usually adding to the spice of the show. The show used to be from about 2pm to 4pm. You could practically forget all your problems within those two hours. The night time, from 7pm, gets to bring my best sport crew known as *Femi and the Gang* on board, with the sport show known as *Game On.* They effortless make sport analyses and commentaries easy. I had always admired them for their high level of excellence and dedication towards ensuring that millions of people get to be aware of sport activities round the world. The initial team was made up of Bolarinwa Olajide, Bimbo Awoyele, Emmanuel Etim, Olisa Chukwuma, Kelechi Nwosu, Kelechi Nkoro, Deji Faremi, Princess Fiona, Okon 'Ediye' Nya and the boss, Femi Obong-

Daniels. They also had an early morning show known as *Sports Drive*. Personally, *Femi and the Gang* were the biggest reason why I got stuck with *Nigeria info* most times due to the live commentaries of English Premiership matches, UEFA Champions League matches, as well as football matches of the Super Eagles and Super Falcons of Nigeria. I also remember listening to them as the Super Eagles lifted the Africa Cup of Nations for the third time in 2013.

These experiences made me see the radio as an invaluable friend of the people. I also got to like several On-Air Personalities during this period, and wondered if I would not end up either being one, or at least, get married to one.

Retirees' Contemplations

Iya Risi's Buka [1] is just at the second turn of *Ekundayo street,* close to *Ansar-ud-deen* Grammar School, Badagry, Lagos state. This eatery is painted brown, with sketchy patches of black. It is one of the popular spots in this community, converging people of all ages. It was said to have been built ten years ago, when Iya Risi decided to venture into this business having gotten enough customers during her baking days. She is now a cordon bleu chef, with over eight active staff working under her. The interior of *Iya Risi's Buka* is a mix of locally made furniture and well-placed electrical devices, such as two standing fans and a big flat screen television. There are also sections for drinks and pastries, as well as an exclusive place where *isi-ewu* [2], *nkwobi* [3] and palm wine are served. Flashes of artistic brilliance are visibly seen on the walls too, with graphite and charcoal drawings of abstract origins. Consequently, this *buka* is a safe place for people to dock and rest from the ill winds of life, acting as the palm trees and fresh air of the islands for the bricks and mortar of the city. Some people in the community still suggest that the name should be changed from *Iya Risi's Buka* to *Iya Risi's Restaurant,* as its capacity is now more than a local-side eatery. Students pay homage to this iconic centre before going to school, nourishing their buccal cavities or eventually buying food for later hours. The unemployed male youths see it as a place to discuss about the football matches of the week, and quite frankly, they rub minds on the betting tips and odds of different betting organizations. Those employed tend to buy food from this place either regularly or when they feel too tired to prepare a meal. Primarily, it is the elderly men who tend to meet more frequently at *Iya Risi's Buka*. They come from nearby houses with almost empty stomachs and strange expressions. It started as a once in a week kind of meeting until the uniformity of their stories turned it to an everyday convergence, except for Sundays, when they worship the Most High in their churches and houses.

Mr. Osagie, also known as *Daddy James* is always the earliest to come. He walks with a certain kind of easiness, albeit he has a protruding stomach. It is widely known that he had worked with the Osun state civil service for 35 years, retiring as a principal of one of the state owned secondary schools at the age of 58. He is well respected in the community, especially for his leadership role in the construction of two boreholes and the purchase of a new transformer. He was in charge of the contribution, going from house to house, and ensuring that every working class person contributed to the projects. To many, he is a father who should be on the honour rolls of humanity. The others- Mr. Femi, Mr. Okafor, Mr. Segun, Mr. Yusuf and Mr. Eneramo, all worked under the Federal Government before retiring. Mr. Femi and Mr. Okafor are both 65 years, while Mr. Segun, Mr. Yusuf and Mr. Eneramo are 68 years old. Mr. Osagie is the oldest, having lived for 70 years so far. They all have families, except Mr. Segun, who decided to be a celibate from his tender years. He is also a man of many words, being as sharp as a razor in a barber shop.

Today, they meet like fellow comrades in misery, with usual zeal to talk about their pension fund saga. The sun is gradually giving way to the gathering stormy clouds in this windy Monday afternoon. *Iya Risi's buka* is slightly filled up, even as the retirees take their places at their favorite spot. The conversion starts as the thunders begin to get louder.

Mr. Segun: This rain will be heavy o.

Mr. Yusuf: It is good that it falls, the heat has been too much.

Mr. Segun: *Abi o*[4].

Mr. Okafor: So, any news on this month's pension?

Mr. Segun: Ah! No news o. It is already the 28th day of this month, and nothing still seems to be happening.

Mr. Eneramo: *They will still pay us naw* [5], let us have patience.

Mr. Yusuf: I think so too, or have you finished the one they sent last month?

Mr. Okafor: Yes o. You know my own pension is not much. I retired as a driver and apart from my self-employed driving job, this pension is what keeps me going.

Daddy James: So what will I say about myself? You know that I am not part of this contributory pension scheme, the one they call CPS. It is the state government that pays me directly, unlike you people that have pension fund administrators who play a major part. As at now, there is no retiree of the Osun state government that has been paid for the past 3 months. Thank God for my children who send me money monthly. Only God knows how I would have been looking by now.

Mr. Yusuf: I heard that people even protested last week about it, but nothing was done, instead, they were dispersed by policemen.

Daddy James: So true. Let us just wait and see what will happen. As for me, I have even given up on this pension thing. Those of us who never had the privilege to be part of the CPS are usually treated like we never even worked for the government in the first place. I heard of my fellow Osun state retiree who just died last month because of hardship. It was said that he was working at a construction site when he just fell down and died, you can just imagine that. Some of us are even paid 1000-naira a month as pension *o,* and the current electricity bill is now double the former price. I still pity those of us who retired under the defined-benefit plan, as both the state and local governments keep having a nonchalant attitude towards us. Most times, they tell us that there is no money on ground to pay pensioners.

Mr. Eneramo: *Nawa o* [6]. So this is what you people go through.

Daddy James: My brother, *na so we dey see am o* [7]. Unlike your CPS, that contributions are made by you and your employer, *for this defined-benefit plan ehn* [8], it is only the employer that makes the contribution towards the pension. There is also no intervening pension fund administrator to help us out, so we are always at the mercy of the government.

Mr. Segun: Ah! This thing is even more serious than I thought.

Daddy James: *Yes o,* it truly is. *Another thing there is that for us in the former pension scheme sef [9],* we are always required to come for continuous reverification exercise so that they can be sure that we are still alive. If we do not come for the reverification process every year, we will not be paid whenever they decide to finally pay us.

Mr. Yusuf: *So what if person die nko? [10]*

Daddy James: In that case, that will be the end o. Nothing *sef* will be given to the family, they will just close the payment completely for that person without even providing any support for the family members. It is just so sad. I pray that God will help us in this our country.

The rain finally starts to fall. *Iya Risi's buka* is now filled up with people seeking to take refuge from the heavy downpour. The conversation continues on pension issues, then gradually, it gives way to memories of their working days in the civil service. They talk further of how they used to be loyal to their heads of departments and cover up for the misdemeanours of other workers. Mr. Segun goes on to tell his compeers of how he was able to keep himself from *Delilahs* and *Jezebels,* who all wanted to spoil his celibacy anointing. Daddy James also shares his experiences of being a principal. They all smile, nod or laugh at the different stories of one another, while devouring the served amala with

52

egusi soup. They ask for palm wine too, and then drink to the memoirs in their hearts.

It thunders on and rains even harder until the voice of the rain becomes louder than their individual voices. This makes them to stop talking, as no one can be heard clearly. Then, one by one, with palm-wine-filled cups, their minds wander to their past, while waiting for the rain to come to its end.

---

1 A kind of local restaurant.

2 Goat's head soup.

3 A Nigerian dish made from cow foot.

4 yes o.

5 Confident of the payment that is to come.

6 A way of implying that a situation is quite serious or tiring.

7 It is what it is.

8 To make emphasis.

9 To emphasize a point/issue.

10 What if someone dies?

Badagry Heritage Museum

Copyright: travelwaka

I knew Taiwo and Kehinde from nursery one at ASCON Staff School, Topo, Badagry. They were non-identical twins with such a friendly spirit. They lived inside the ASCON complex. I still remember the days when I would go to their house frequently to play while on my way to my parents' offices, who were both working in ASCON. On some days, I would stand and jump on the sofa of their sitting room. This usually caused Taiwo to be quite worried as he was always warned by his parents not to allow anyone perform any form of acrobatics or gravity defying moves on the sofa. I was just so fond of the twins. I continued going to their house to play until a particular week that I was flogged on two consecutive days by my dad. The first beating came on the evening of the day that I was sent on an errand by a worker in my mum's office (Mrs. Lateef). The errand required that I had to pass through the house of this twins. It happened that they were playing with other nearby friends at that point. I recall that I actually forgot about the errand, and joined the game they were playing. I continued playing to the point that the woman who sent me on the errand had to come around that area to know what was delaying me from coming back to the office. That was how she saw me playing with my friends, with her message undelivered. My mum and subsequently, my dad got to hear about this. I faced the music when I got back home, and was duly beaten with a cane by my dad. The same scenario repeated itself the next day, this time, I went to the house of my brother's friend in ASCON complex. I went to play the popular *300 in 1 CD game*[1], only for me to hear that my father was at the door. I was shocked to say the least. I was beaten again when I got home that day. That was how I stopped going to people's houses to play.

I had other great childhood friends such as Israel Igiebor, who was one of the fastest pupils in my class. I still remember when we were playing in primary 2, and I mistakenly ran into a class filled with students who were doing a choreography for an upcoming *Speech and Prize-giving Day.* The teacher in charge of the choreography was Mrs. Anabor. I remember her being so angry with me, wondering how I could be so carefree as to disrupt a choreography session. She gave me strokes of cane on random parts of my body in quite a disgraceful way. It was truly one to never forget.

Most of my classmates in primary school were my friends, the likes of Kotin Michael, Ojora Kole, Adewunmi Theophilus, Tosin, Sulaimon Ibrahim, Joshua Bassey, Elizabeth Bassey, Adeola David, Oriola John, Osagiede Precious, Omole Israel, Akeem, Hunge, Matthew, and a whole lot more.

Joshua Bassey and I used to have several running lessons together while we waited for our elder sisters in primary 6 to close. His elder sister was Patience. Theophilus and I were quite close even up to JSS1. We used to talk about various Christian subjects, and preached the gospel too. We both did this until I left Badagry Junior Grammar School, just after JSS1. There was also this interesting game we used to play that we called *Catcher.* It was all about a set of people who would be "Catching" another set of people. It was my favourite game, and the most played by my primary school friends too. I liked it as it involved running, and diverse ways of either outsmarting the catcher or catching someone. It was just like an adumbration of the legendary Nigerian childhood game known as *Police and Thief.*

I went on to have several friends in my secondary school days, the likes of Abraham, Jimoh Kazeem, Nwokolo Chukwuma, Okunnu Lawal, Ebivwie Great, Vann Paul, Solaja Sonyaolu, Suleimon Mukhtar, Tafa Zainab, Ambunga Lisa, Aisha, Ahmadu, Ayomide, Dike Cindy, Kingsmike Martha, Halim Mary, Agenge Enawayon, Obaado Benjamin, Iranloye Mayowa, Opeoluwa Campbell, Sunmola Samiat, Orajekwe Lilian, Kolapo Tobi, amongst several others who made my stay in secondary school quite memorable. There were always times when I would play football with several of my mates after terminal examinations. This was something that I always looked forward to, as it served as my own way of easing the stress of the cumbersome school work.

Kazeem still remains one of the funniest people I have ever come across. I met him while in JSS1. He was also one of the most outstanding students in JSS1C in Badagry Junior Grammar School in 2007/2008 academic session. Then Mukhtar was the only student I never did beat academically all through my secondary school days. I met him in JSS2 at French Village International College, Ajara, Badagry. He was by all means a very serious student who also loved a bit of football and sprinting. Enawayon was a friend and rival from SS1 to SS3. I met him at Ascension College. I still remember the first Further-mathematics assignment that we were given. He came out tops, scoring 5 marks out of 5 questions, leaving the rest of the class to gather less scores. He was also a good footballer.

There was a certain day when all the boys in my class played football non-stop for about two hours. We were in SS1 then, just before the third term examination. We came for two makeshift lectures on topics in both Agricultural science and Chemistry. We took a break after the Agricultural Science lecture. The break was supposed to be for just 10-15 minutes, but we ended up playing football for two hours, to the dismay of the chemistry teacher, Mrs. Avoseh. In the end, we never attended that particular chemistry class. We were flogged on the following Monday morning, and given a sizeable portion of grass to clear. I remember how it felt to have the main school field for ourselves for those two hours; we were just too excited on that particular Saturday afternoon. It was during that day that I saw the dance steps of Enawayon too, as he tried to act out a popular comedy skit while waiting for his *set* [2] to play again. It was also on that day that I looked unto the skies and told my Creator to help me never forget all the events that had played out before my eyes. It was simply an amazing day.

At other times, Gbenga and Chukwudi would come to my house to play PlayStation 2, which I had when I was in senior secondary school. We also had times when we would go to a nearby *Game centre* [3], either around our area or close to the school. We would either pay individually for each game or do *Loser pay* [4].

Daniel, Baba, Bukoh David, Sandra, Peter, Petrov, Abayomi, Ladan Fidosi, Prevailar, Segun, Ifeanyi, Adeboye Stephen, Eni Michael, Alivide Michael, Azeezat, Lukman, and Olaitan, will always be cherished.

1 A CD game that was once popular.

2 A group of players selected to play per time.

3 A place where video games are played.

4 A scenario whereby the loser of a video game match gets to pay the fee for himself, as well as that of his game partner in a game centre/shop.

"High" by *Lighthouse Family* is still my favourite love song. It is a classic from the musical duo-Tunde Baiyewu and Paul Tucker. Tunde Baiyewu is the vocalist, while Paul Tucker serves as the keyboard maestro. It is widely believed that Tunde Baiyewu is a stepson of the former military leader and president of Nigeria, Mr. Olusegun Obasanjo. *Lighthouse Family* are also well known for other songs like "Lifted", "Ocean Drive", "Lost in Space", "Ain't No Sunshine" and "Raincloud". At a point, the song "High" reached number one on the *Australian Singles Chart.* I also grew up listening to songs by *Backstreet boys, Styl-Plus* and *Westlife,* amongst other old school love songs by Lionel Richie, *The Commodores,* Ben E. King, Whitney Houston, Stevie Wonder, Billy Ocean, Phil Collins, Michael Bolton, Percy Sledge, Mariah Carey, Cyndi Lauper, The Jackson 5 and Celine Dion. I was well loaded with lyrics and rhymes from these songs, waiting for the perfect day to skillfully unleash them on the right female being.

I tried to give no room for relationships in my teenage years, doing my best to study hard and be the good boy I was largely expected to be. I followed the instructions of my parents, presbyters, bishops, pastors, prophets and prophetesses. The only problem here was that I had started noticing a change in my physical perception of every girl that I saw. I could gradually get to tell if a female was beautiful in form and appearance, a phenomenon I could not explain. Nature continued doing its biological work as the testosterone levels in my body surged higher. I became more aware of myself and the opposite gender. My eyes opened to the world, as I wrestled with the demands of my new body and the tenets of my faith. The only restraint to having a girlfriend became my parents, as I would end up asking myself "What if my parents get to find out that I have a girlfriend? Where would I start the explanation from?" So, I had to resist every voice that would say "Arise, pursue and go after that girl". I knew that I would be in serious trouble if my parents get to find out about any relationship escapade. It was this fear that kept me till JSS3.

In that particular class, it happened that a chocolate-skinned girl named Victoria had *feelings* for me. Before then, I was already getting rave reviews in school, as everyone thought I was quite brilliant. Victoria was truly beautiful, an angelic being in human form. Her smile could melt the hearts of a thousand strong men, and her poise could make her a superstar on the runway. She was a poet and even though I had not really started writing at that point, I still looked forward to hearing her poetic renditions on significant days of the school, as I was always fascinated by her calm and soothing words, etched in pure bliss and furnished with graceful aplomb. I used to help her out with some difficult mathematics questions, explaining some of the abstruse concepts to her. That was how we started seeing each other during the regular school breaks, either solving questions or talking about J.K. Rowling's *Harry Potter*, a name she was also fond of calling me due to the spectacles I was using for myopia. She went on to call herself *Hermione Granger,* the name of Harry Potter's female friend. It went on like this till SS1. Then things got a little messy as it seemed like she had expected me to had asked her out, a situation I was really never considering. All I think I wanted was friendship, but it turned out that she wanted more than that. I had to make swift moves, telling her the exact thing on my mind after which the closeness between us was never the same again. We still remained friends and acted only as such through the remaining days in secondary school. My male folks always wondered why I never did accept her as a potential girlfriend. I also wondered too, as any male student in my set would have been the happiest person in the world to have her as a *bae* [1]. Apart from my parents, I still do not know why I held back from further proceedings with her. Could it be that I was just scared of any form of commitment at that time?

Or was I already thinking of the future, and the possibility of marrying her? Maybe I was just confused too.

Behind the scenes was another girl, one that I had come to know on a rather disturbing note. She always seemed to dislike me. She was brainy, exceptionally good in most subjects. She was also a poet, more vocal and yet calm, shy but also courageous. She was a fine blend of several ambivalent qualities. Her name was Ruth. She had the eyes of an enchantress and the beauty of the biblical Queen Esther. I always wanted to know why she did not like me, and why she was always verbally going against me. In the process of doing this, I got more than I had bargained for. I got to see her for who she really was; a sweet soul who only thought that I was proud and arrogant. I got to apologise for my attitude and misdeeds, even though I did not fully agree to all her complaints. The events that followed that day were quite surprising. I started noticing that we had more similarities, from passion to faith, from worldviews to attitudes. I gradually became like one under the spell of her love, precisely my love for her. I forgot about the instructions of my parents, as I could not explain what was going on the inside of me. I began to look forward to seeing her every day in school, to the point that I would never feel comfortable in class unless she was around. There were other times I would leave one of the laboratories just to go in search of her around the school, as if she was a missing person. I had never felt like this before as I was captured into the passionate realm of love. My grades progressively started dropping, but I was undeterred as I continued to follow the burning passion of love. I learnt from William Shakespeare's "Romeo and Juliet", that *Romeo* paid the ultimate price for love, even as the bible tells me the same about the Messiah. All these made me to surge further, as I asked myself "What therefore is academics compared to love?" I became a motivational speaker to her and a great fan of the *Song of Solomon* [2], even as *Westlife* songs kept coming to my mind whenever I thought about her, maybe she was the queen of my heart and I was flying without wings, from coast to coast, as I laid my love on her. I started sending messages to her through the phone at day and at night, motivating and inspiring her each day and more at weekends. I was in love and that was all that mattered to me. We would further chat on *2go* [3], where she would ask me if she was beautiful. I would then reply her by typing "You are the fairest of a million maidens, and your beauty is like the heat from the sun and the wind from the north, the blind and deaf can attest to it". By SS2 and SS3, we were already exchanging handwritten letters almost every day, talking about our faith, our different families and of course, the love we shared for each other. She lured me to fall in love with poetry and turned me into a poet too, a feat Victoria was unsuccessful at. My scores got worse in some subjects as I preferred thinking about her to my studies. In the first term of SS3, I wrote my further-mathematics exam just immediately after spending about 2 hours with her. She had stopped taking this subject in SS2 as it was no longer compulsory. I entered that exam hall full of both love and fear, love for Ruth, and fear for my further-maths exam. I still ended up doing quite well in that exam.

I love happy endings, but sadly, this one did not turn out that way. She loved me all along, but she was not ready to be in a relationship with me at that point. I was confused. In one of her handwritten letters, she wrote that she could not be in any romantic relationship at that stage of her life. I did not get to know what her reasons were; neither was I able to place my hands on what the problem might had been. We went on acting like everything was fine on the outside, chatting in the same manner as we had always done, but I was in severe pain on the inside. I hoped that things would have change before we left secondary school, but that never happened. We kept on having back and forth contemplations even after our school days, as emotions went high every now and then. We eventually had to settle for being just friends, *friend-zoning* [4] each other like no mutual feeling ever existed. It all felt like an extended payback of what had happened between Victoria and I.

---

1 Girlfriend.

2 A book of the Bible.

3 A free mobile social networking application.

4 Being only friends with someone that might be (or might have been) a girlfriend/boyfriend.

Love's Metaphors

I. Love is a coin
Choose both sides.

II. Love is a drama
It has a stage, and curtains do fall.

III. Love is a trigger-happy policeman
It takes no prisoners.

IV. Love is what comes to your mind
When you see *Senami* [1] blushing at the words of her lover.

V. Love is a fire
It can be reckless.

---

1 An Egun name for a female, meaning "Gift from God".

Point of No Return, Badagry Slave Route

Copyright: face2faceafrica

My birthplace was Badagry, in a hospital popularly known as *Marina clinic.* It was located close to the Badagry post office, along the road that leads to the Badagry prison, slave trade museum, market, and the first storey building in Nigeria. I still remember the bed I was laid on as a baby; I got to know that it was also the same bed that my brother and sister were laid on during their tender years too. That bed is still in the house, as my mum does not have any plan to give it out any time soon; she holds on to it dearly.

We started life in Badagry in the classical *Face me I face you* house. We had moved to Badagry from a place known as *Itire* in Lagos state on account of my dad's work in the civil service. My dad always tells us of how he saw a straight road in one of his dreams on one of the nights he was asking God for his opinion about coming to Badagry. It turned out to be God's decision, as he saw the replica of his dream when he came to Badagry. This particular *Face me I face you* house was popularly called *Borobo house.* It was directly opposite a certain Assemblies of God Church, which was also close to a shrine. It had no gate and no water supply system. We had to use the pit latrine too, coupled with fetching water from well, and drinkable water from a house we used to call *Black gate*. We called it *Black gate* as that was also the colour of the gate of the building where we used to get drinkable water or *Drinking water* as we used to call it back then. *Black gate* was also slightly far from *Borobo house,* a distance of about 300m.

Borobo house was very exciting, as my siblings and I played with the children of our neighbours. I still remember a certain mini-birthday celebration for my sister in *Borobo house,* and how we took pictures with cake, *coke* and *fanta. Borobo house* was also not devoid of occasional arguments and quarrels, just as most *Face me I face you houses.* Our neighbours included Papa Shina, Mama Shina, Auntie Aina, Mama Alaba, Papa Seyi, alongside their family members and sometimes, friends. Seyi, the son of Papa Seyi later opened a game centre, where I would later play *PlayStation2* with my friends, and also buy game discs by the time I got to senior secondary school. He later went on to open a football viewing centre, where the youths would gather to watch live matches of the Super Eagles, English Premier League, UEFA Champions League, La Liga, Africa cup pf Nations, UEFA Euro cup, Copa America, and other interesting cup tournaments. There was also a nearby house simply known as *Mama Paul place,* where my mum used to take me to in the morning before going to work, as I was too small to start going to school at that time. Mama Paul was an agile, smart and responsible woman who was well known around that area. She would take care of me as well as other children until our parents would come back from work. This continued until my parents enrolled me in ASCON Staff School in the year 2000.

We moved on to rent another apartment in the early 2000s. This time, it was a 3-bedroom flat. It was located quite close to the *Borobo house.* This was my home address, from about primary 1 to my 4th year in the University. It was more comfortable for a family of five. The bus stop was *White house, Agankameh,* while the name of the house was *Oyerinde House.* The Landlady was known as Mrs. Oyerinde, a dark-skinned elderly woman, who only comes around in December to collect her house rent for the year. Most events in this book took place while I was living in this house. We had neighbours like Papa Godiah, Mama Stephen, Mama Ada, Mama Salvation, Mama Sewedon, Auntie Gloria, Mr. Agu, Papa Olumide, Mr. Okey, together with their family members and friends.

I remember ASCON and ASCON Staff School, where I had both my nursery and primary school education. The memories are countless, from having a fractured hand to my graduation ceremony in nursery two, where I recited "I am letter 'N', 'N' for Nurse...", while Oketola Taiwo recited "I am letter 'L', 'L' for Lion...". I also started out in a rather sloppy manner, trying my best to do well academically. I was quite a slow learner who loved to play very often. I later started cheating during tests, especially in certain subjects like Home-Economics and Social Studies. Our tests were usually done at the back of our notebooks, this enabled me to carefully turn to the front of the book during tests, look at the answers to the questions, and then write my answers at the back of the notebook. I did this from around primary 3 to the first term of primary 5, when I finally stopped such acts.

I remember how Sulaimon Ibrahim never dropped out of the best 3 students across the three arms of each class throughout our stay in primary school. Something strange later happened in primary 4, when a certain Desmond Inyang took all the prizes in the Speech and prize-giving day, except the prizes for the best student in Islamic Religious Knowledge and that of the Christian Religious Knowledge; I took the latter. That particular day was a very sad one for me as I thought I would be called upon in the midst of everyone to come and receive my prize. The event had to be stopped at a particular point before my name could be called, as it was getting late. This meant that I had to be given my prize in a private manner, from

Mrs. Gandonu, in the first term of primary 5. That particular Speech and Prize-giving day served as a major turning point in my life, especially in terms of my academics. That event had the presence of the Director General of ASCON and other top dignitaries of the establishment. My father was also present on that day. He came to see me perform a rendition on the late Military dictator, General Sani Abacha. I was given the piece by Mr. Amosu, and a fancy eyeglass to put on too, just like the one of the late military head of state. My parents had helped me in the preparation for that recitation. I was also given a letter by the school authorities to my parents, telling them that I would be given a prize on the Speech and Prize-giving day of that year. I was looking forward to be called on that day, with my dad on ground. The first, second and third positions were eventually announced for each class. I was not called to the podium, meaning that I had to step aside. I still recall hearing the voice of Mr. Amosu, telling the other students around that area "If you want to be like them, read your book". He kept on shouting this while using his cane to disperse the students who were still around the area where the first, second, and third students for each class were sitting. I cried that day, feeling sad that my dad was present at that event and saw another person go home with all the prizes. In the midst of this tearful episode, I made up my mind to get the prize for the overall best student for the next class, primary 5. This meant that I had to beat the likes of Ibrahim, Taiwo, Kotin Michael, Precious Osagiede, Ojora Kole, Elizabeth Bassey, and a certain Adeola David.

Adeola David was a pastor's son, a very handsome one at that. He started attending ASCON Staff School in Primary 5 as his father was posted to one of the branches of his church in Badagry. He proved to be extremely brilliant, even more than us all. All was already looking bright for him to assume the overall best student in primary 5 before a drastic change occurred, one that helped me. His father was surprisingly posted again to Ota, Ogun state. This led to him leaving the school in second term of primary 5. I did not really know how I felt at that stage, as I really liked him as a friend, yet I knew his going would open the door for me to get the first position. He left the school on a Friday, sadly, it was also a day that had its own troubles. It happened that some students had reported that we had been using a popular *biro-tapping game* for gambling. This led to the flogging of everyone that had been an active player of that game. Though the majority of us never played that game for gambling purposes, we were still flogged, as the school authorities spared no one. I remember that I was among the first set of students to be flogged by the French teacher, Mr. Abdul. David too was flogged, alongside my other friends. We were all sad that day. It was really not the kind of goodbye that David would have loved to have. I went on to take first position in primary 5, with Sulaimon Ibrahim and Osagiede Precious coming second and third respectively. It was one of my best days on earth as I was so honoured, together with my parents too.

I also recall how my siblings and I used to enter *Topo buses* [2] and school bus on some days before my dad bought a car. I still remember how popular those *Topo buses* were, and how people used to lap as well as sit on a part of the bus we used to call *Engine,* for a reduced cost of transportation. I still remember most of my primary school teachers, Mrs. Obawoye, Mrs. Oguniyi, Mr. Oni, Mrs. Oguntodu, Mrs. Offem, Mrs. Dosunmu, Mrs. Hassan, Mr. Etu, Mrs. Gege, Mr. Makpo, Mrs. Olufade, and my great headmaster, Mr. Ajape.

Growing up, I remember the first time we bought a generator. It was the popular *I better pass my neighbour,* the small *Tiger* generator. I recall how the engineer wrestled with the connection while trying to do a changeover, with my brother helping him out. I remember how I would follow my parents to work daily in my dad's car. I recall all the cassettes that my brother bought for the car, the likes of *Shout to the Lord kids,* Igbo gospel songs, and classic gospel songs from the 90's and early 2000s. I got exposed to many old gospel songs through this means.

My dad's car was the legendary *Toyota Carina II.* I still recall the day that car was bought. It was brought into the compound in the morning of a certain weekday through the help of one of our neighbours, who was quite a high-ranking police officer around the Seme border area, he was popularly called *Papa Godia,* Godia is the name of his first child, a female. I remember how Ismaila worked on that car at a place called *Idale,* still in Badagry. Ismaila was our first mechanic, a gentle one.

I recollect how my brother started buying movies and seasonal films for us to watch, together with how my mother bought us *Westlife* collections. My sister and I would go out to rent movies on countless occasions. The movies were all Nollywood, where we got to know the likes of Chioma Chukwuka, Emeka Ike, Justice Esiri, Ejike Asiegbu, Eni Edo, the funny duo of *Aki* and *Pawpaw,* amongst several Nollywood stars at that time. My brother and sister were also responsible for making me love old school music as they constantly bought cassettes and discs of several old school artistes. My love for Highlife and Juju music started in my mum's office in a certain department in ASCON, as there was a tall man who constantly played songs by Chief Commander Ebenezer Obey, Sir Victor Olaiya, and King Sunny Ade, through one of the computers in the office. The name of that man was Mr. Titus, who was also my mum's co-worker. Then, I recall how my brother and I started playing the *300 in 1 CD game,* and then migrated to *Terminator, Sega, PlayStation1* and finally *PlayStation2.* My mother was instrumental in buying most of these games. I still remember that she bought *PlayStation1* from a certain man named Ballak in Badagry market. Ballak was also a major distributor of electrical gadgets to ASCON Staff when he was alive. He died, with the cause of death linked to black magic, which was widely believed to have been used against him. My dad was the one who bought the *PlayStation2.*

We used to buy bread at a place known as *Oropo.* I was the person sent most times to get the bread. The way to *Oropo* also goes through a Chemist shop, who we usually get our medications from. He was a very friendly man. The road to *Oropo* gets flooded during the rainy season, meaning that we had to walk through the water on those days. We also had the night-market around that area, where we bought vegetables like *Ugu, green* and other things for food. There was also a mechanic shop at the other entrance of the road leading to our house, just opposite a police barrack, that was where Mr. Akeem used to work. Mr. Akeem was our second mechanic who also doubled as our driver on days when we needed to make early trips to cities inside Lagos. He was a good man.

I went to four secondary schools- Frontline School, Badagry Junior Grammar School, French Village International College, and Ascension College. All these schools gave me different exposures, adding to my educational background in more ways than one. I remember many of those teachers, as well as the friends I made in those schools.

I visited the Badagry slave trade museum on one occasion with students from different schools, where we saw different heartbreaking collections, images, and sculptures, with a view of the *Point of no return.* It was said that any slave who got to that point on the lagoon never returned home again. It was at this point that shipment of the slaves was done.

I got to start using the Badagry library in SS3, together with Oyedeji Oluwafemi, Seun Coker, God-service, Abraham and Sesede. I have never entered the first storey building in Nigeria even though I had become accustomed to seeing it from a close distance. I heard that inside it lies the table and chair of the late Bishop Samuel Ajayi Crowther, who translated the Bible from English to Yoruba language. It is also speculated that this building was erected by Reverend Henry Townsend of the Church Missionary Society. The foundation of the structure was said to have been laid in 1842, while the house was completed three years later in 1845.

I later had a health issue with my respiratory system, as I was diagnosed with bronchitis Pneumonia while in JSS2, which made me to have asthma-like attack on two occasions. One of such occasions was in school, the other was just after I had returned from the market with my parents. I almost died on those two occasions, as I found it difficult to breath. I had to go for X-ray and was subsequently given tablets and injections at the *Sacred Heart Catholic hospital,* close to the Badagry market. I started using eyeglass in JSS3 for myopia, and I also had Chickenpox in SS2, which was quite a bad experience.

I always hated summer lesson during the long vacation after third term. I had always believed that it was stressful enough going to school every day for three terms, and did not know why there should be another summer lesson when the children should actually be playing at home or learning a skill. I had no option though than to go for these lessons in a nearby school as my parents deemed it necessary. Most times, I was beaten by teachers during the summer lesson, and on one occasion, I was slapped by a teacher. All these made me to question the usefulness of summer lessons.

I wrote my General Certificate Examination (GCE) in Topo Grammar School. The school is just beside ASCON. It was exciting getting to see several faces who all had the same exams to write. I recall the days when *expos*[3] would be given from the hands of invigilators, and how some students would be called to another classroom for special attention and extra tutorials in the midst of a serious exam. At other times, some people would come to read the supposed answers of the objective questions, and would then ask us to quickly shade those answers and submit. I even saw my one-time private chemistry teacher during one of the exams. He came to write the chemistry alternative-to-practical examination for another person. He comfortably wrote that exam and even extended his hand of fellowship to other students who were willing and obedient to succeed through that means. I saw part of the decadence of the education sector of Nigeria, which was also a reflection of what the country was, and still is. Coincidentally, I also wrote my Joint Admissions and Matriculation Board (JAMB) exam in Topo Grammar School. This time, the level of examination malpractice was on a higher level, as some of the officials and invigilators offered the answers of the different question types to the people. This happened about 10 minutes after some officials from the JAMB office came to carry out a hurried inspection; they seemed like they had several places to go to on that day. I remember being the last person to leave that classroom, as even the invigilator had to say "*I pray make you do well as you no use expo*"[4]. I actually did not do that well in the JAMB exam, but it was sufficient for me to be invited for the Post-Unified Tertiary Matriculation Examination (Post-UTME) of the Premier university in Nigeria, where I was subsequently given admission to study Pharmacy.

I remember how everyone in the family went to the Freeman Memorial Methodist Church in Badagry, popularly believed to be the first Methodist Church in Nigeria. It was named after Thomas Birch Freeman, who was an Anglo-African missionary, and the first Methodist minister to arrive Nigeria, stepping foot in the muddy creeks of Badagry on September 24, 1842. Though there were several ways to the church, we would always pass through the route that enabled us to see the First Storey Building in Nigeria. It proved to be the shortest route. We would also pass through the Badagry library, the Badagry post office, Brazilian Barracoon, Holy Innocent School and the House of the Mobee of Badagry. The Mobee of Badagry was a prominent chief who was well involved in the slave trade business in the 19th century. It was said that the slaves were sold in a market known as the vlekete market in Badagry, and that at least, 300 slaves were sold on each vlekete market day, which could make up to about 17,000 slaves on a yearly basis. Items such as mirror, canon gun, gun powder and the likes were exchanged for humans, a deal in which Chief Mobee was said to have been involved in. It was also said that the eldest son of the Mobee was not in agreement with his father's decision about slave trade. The Mobee's son later made a successful attempt at stopping slave trade in Badagry when he ascended the throne, with the help of the missionaries. One can surely visit the Badagry Slave Trade Museum and the Mobee Royal Family Slave Museum when in Badagry to see most of the pictures, materials, items and sculptures of how the slave trade used to be in Badagry. The contents of the two museums can be both heartrending and unbelievable.

We usually get to park the car close to the palace of the *Oba* [5] of Badagry, who also attends Methodist Church with his family. The Methodist Church Sunday service usually runs from 7:30am to 9:00am, for the English service. The Yoruba service starts immediately, and then the Egun service follows through, except for the Sundays when it would be a Combined Service, which usually starts by 10am. The service always gets started with the opening hymn, then the prayer, which would be followed by the praise and worship session, first and second scripture reading came next, closely followed by the sermon, then another time for prayers, followed by the offering and announcement before the benediction and recessional hymn, then we finally get to hear "The Lord be with you", and we would reply the presbyter by saying "And also with you". We would then exchange pleasantries with other church members before we would go home. I also got to love hymns during this period. I found them to be an expression of both art and divinity. My dad taught me how to sing some of the hymns. My favourite hymns were *The Great Physician* (by William Hunter) and *Gentle Jesus, Meek and Mild* (by Charles Wesley, who was the brother of John Wesley, the founder of Methodist Church).

I once did something quite mischievous in church. It happened during one of those Sundays when we would do what is known as *Children Harvest.* On that particular occasion, I had no money for the offering, and I was also one of the children close to the altar of the church on that Sunday. I ended up not dropping any money in the offering box even though I had extended my hand into it, in essence, I dropped nothing for God. My parents were far away in the congregation, and I was not sure of their location too. All these made me to act in that manner. I felt bad for a long time though, wondering why I never rushed down in search of my parents before the offering time. I can still remember the humble Bishop, cheerful presbyters, hardworking reverends, serious lay-preachers, dedicated ushers, and other esteemed workers of that Badagry diocese.

I later attended Revival Fire of the End Time Ministries, popularly called REFEM in Badagry. It was quite an unorthodox church, with more similarities to the Pentecostal churches around. It was very close to the house, and my parents also granted me the permission to attend the church. I later joined the workers of the church, becoming a chorister. I did very badly as a chorister, even though my choir mistress was quite lenient with me, encouraging me to do better. I usually could neither sing tenor nor soprano well, though it looked like alto was the part my voice was best suited for, yet, I still sang off-key most times. I only remember taking the Praise and Worship session only twice, and co-led the choir ministration just once. I felt I was a terrible singer and wondered why I did not join a different unit at an earlier stage. That aside, I got to know the extent of spiritual terms like deliverance, anointing and prophecy more in REFEM. It was also here that I got scared of ladies, as it looked like there were more ladies that would fall under the anointing than men during deliverance. I feared that many ladies were in some kind of bondage or demonic oppression. I can also recollect most of the people in REFEM, including the pastors, deliverance ministers, choristers, ushers, and prophetess (Mrs.) Akinkugbe (we popularly called her Mummy, Mummy Fire or Mummy Akinkugbe). She truly took me as a son, and helped me to be a better person both in character and in the Christian faith; she remains legendary. I also got my first guitar during this time, as my dad bought one for me.

There was this Umuahia meeting that my parents used to attend every 2nd Sunday of the month around 4pm. The meeting was for those who were from Umuahia in Abia state but reside in Badagry. I had to follow them to these meetings as I was the only child at home; my siblings were in higher institutions during that period. I recall how the meeting usually proceeded. The talks and comments were usually long, with each person wanting to air his or her view. On one of the end of the year meetings in December, I was appointed as the chairman of the occasion, even though I had no clue on what had been going on in the meetings. However, I enjoyed my special chicken and *jollof* rice on that blessed day.

I remember Mr. Ekokene, who seems to be my dad's closest friend. I also recall Mama Clinton and Mama Ndubuisi who were friends of my mum before their death. I remember them as cool, calm and brave women. There was even a day that Mama Clinton, my mum, and I boarded a motorcycle from ASCON to Iworo-Ajido Model College, Ebute-Olofin, Badagry, to see Clinton and my sister, who were in secondary school at that point. That day will always be memorable.

I would not forget about the talking drum, and how I got to learn about it from few drummers in Badagry. I also remember the first primary school in Nigeria, still located in Badagry. It was first named as *The nursery of infant church,* and later called *St. Thomas Anglican Nursery and Primary school* by Reverend Golmer of the Church Missionary Society. It is currently located at Topo, Badagry, though its initial location was at the site of the first storey building in Nigeria.

Most of my childhood memories can be traced back to this ancient town, serving not just as a reference point for the Trans-atlantic slave trade of the 19th century, but also, as a place where different memoirs were made.

1 A group of one or two-room apartments, with their entrances facing each other along a walkway.

2 Buses that used to go to and fro from Topo Roundabout, Badagry.

3 Materials used for examination malpractice.

4 To pray that I would pass the examination, even without participating in examination malpractice.

5 King.

Bad-agry-ment

I once almost added salt into my tea

Maybe it would had become *sal-tea*

I once ate a full plate of rice on a chair

It was enough for me to become *chair-ful*

Some people say that having an agreement with Badagry people

Is tedious

Others say that it might turn out as a *Bad-agry-ment*

I differ on both.

Appendage

Pizza's Dilemma

The exam hall was as quiet as a graveyard. There was absolute calm as every student tried to write as fast as possible in the three-hour Physiology exam. The course code was *PIO 206,* while its title was *General Physiology II.* It was a 3-unit compulsory course, and the second of a series of Physiology courses to be taken by 200 level Pharmacy students of the University of Ibadan, Ibadan.

I remembered being petrified the first time I saw the course coordinator of the Physiology courses. Her voice had a certain kind of behest, one that earned her both fear and respect. She happened to also be one of the lecturers who taught this particular course, teaching us about the digestive and reproductive systems of the human body. I had no issues with her lectures on reproduction, as we all seemed to understand all the reproductive concepts that she taught us. My predicament started while she was teaching about the digestive system, as there was a certain unpredictability of what her exam questions on digestion would be. This uneasy feeling gradually transcended into the exam hall.

It was a cool Tuesday morning. Everything looked alright from the onset of that day. I had done well to be on time for the start of the exam, doing my last revision and eating in the popular *Zik Cafeteria*[1] before coming to the exam hall. I was really set for the exam. I sat at the front after being one of the first students to enter the exam hall. I also had time to notice that the course coordinator looked unusually beautiful, an adjective I had never used to describe her. I was wondering what was going on, while still trying to place my focus on the exam I was destined to write in a few minutes. Then, the exam started. I quickly read the instructions and browsed through the questions on the exam question paper. That was how I spotted one of her questions on digestion, it went like this "Explain the digestion of *Domino's Pizza*". This was initially supposed to be a good question; my problem here was that I had neither heard of Pizza nor *Domino's Pizza* in my mortal years on planet earth. I had no imagination of what a pizza should be like, let alone *Domino's pizza*. Sadly, this was not my first time of not knowing what most people would perceive as being the norm.

I grew up in a fairly remote area, with no real social centre to visit. The biggest attraction site was a slave trade museum that depicted the Trans-Atlantic slave trade of the 19th century. There was also the historic presence of the first storey building in Nigeria, and a certain Suntan Beach. The available eateries were always that of *buka*[2] and other local side joints, filled with *isi-ewu*[3], *nkwobi*[4] and alcoholic drinks. There were no *Tantalizers, KFC, Mr bigg's, Chicken Republic, Tetrazzini,*

Shoprite, and other mega outlets. This was my bane, as I had little or no physical exposure to such appealing places while growing up. I had to even wonder what an inverter was when I first came to the University of Ibadan for my Post Unified Tertiary Matriculation Examination (Post-UTME), as the person who was to print my large-sized passport photograph said "We have to put on the inverter to print the passport". Then I had quite an experience when I first went to *Tantalizers* in the university. I had programmed my mind to accept the 20-naira per spoon, which was the regular cost in the cafeterias of our halls of residence. I went there with my friends, then I ordered first, a mistake I should not have made. I ordered the normal delicacy I was used to – rice and plantain, only to be shocked that my total bill was 550-naira. At this point, the meal had already been brought forward to me. Then instead of me to start pleading that I did not have that kind of money to spend, I forged head, saying "No, I cannot take it", as if I was negotiating the pay. I was still maintaining my stance before a lady saved me from the impending embarrassment. She just came out of nowhere, and said that she wanted just the same delicacy I had ordered. She took the meal and paid for it, while my local friends and I hurried away, with my friends having a good laugh at me. I felt so bad that day.

Back to the Exam Hall

I did my best to answer all the other questions with a certain kind of precision, finesse and artistry. I was left with only one part of the course coordinator to answer- the part on digestion. This part contained two questions, and we were supposed to answer at least one. The other question was a series of short-answer questions, which I had substantial knowledge on. At the end of my deliberation, I chose to do the right thing by not answering the *Domino's Pizza* question. That meant that I had to answer the series of short-answer questions as fast as I could. I eventually finished writing and submitted my answer booklets just before the end of the exam. I had done the best I could, though, I left the exam hall still feeling like a village man, as I believed *Domino's Pizza* must be popular for it to have been included as part of an exam question. My belief was right, as my friends knew what it was when I asked them after the exam. That was when I made up my mind to have a taste of *Domino's Pizza* after the second semester exams. I was determined to prevent further embarrassing occurrences from happening. I had come to believe that the right exposure is key to one's success, and I never wanted to be denied one again.

---

1 A popular cafeteria in the University of Ibadan, Ibadan.

2 A kind of local restaurant.

3 Goat's head soup.

4 A Nigerian dish made from cow foot.

Every story will glorify the hunter until the lion knows how to write.

- An African Proverb

Acknowledgements

I drew inspiration from *Work Naija: The book of vocations*. It is an amazing art *naija* anthology edited by Otosirieze Obi-Young.

Shop Cogitations was first published in *Kalahari Review.*

Bus Introversion was first published in *Ake Review,* The journal of *Ake Festival* Online, 2021.

Igbinigie Jesuferanmi ensured that this book came to being.

To God Almighty and Father of light, be all the glory and honour.

The Author

Ebisike Chinedum is a Nigerian creative writer, Artist, Graphics designer and Pharmacist. He has had some of his works published in *Ìràwọ̀ Anthology*, CovidHQafrica.com, *Kalahari Review, Ake Review, Uites Write, Syrups and Nebules, Matrix: The Premier*, and *Matrix: La Penultima*. He was one of those shortlisted for the Poets in Nigeria (PIN) *Spoken Word Slam* at the University of Ibadan in 2018. Currently, he writes for *Inkem Arts,* an online Afrocentric literary community. This is his second published book.

Printed in Great Britain
by Amazon

15904882R00063